THIS BO
BELONG

Name:	Age:

Favourite player:

2018/2019
My Predictions...   Actual...

Town's final position:

Town's top scorer:

Championship Winners:

Championship top scorer:

FA Cup Winners:

EFL Cup Winners:

Contributors: Peter Rogers

A TWOCAN PUBLICATION

©2018. Published by twocan under licence from Ipswich Town FC.

ISBN 978-1-912692-28-6

PICTURE CREDITS: Dan Sakal & Warren Page, Grant Pringle, Action Images, Press Association.

£9

CONTENTS

IPSWICH TOWN
FOOTBALL CLUB

MAGICAL
01 DEAN **GERKEN**

GOALKEEPER   DOB: 22/05/1985   COUNTRY: ENGLAND

A towering shot-stopper, Gerken joined the Blues back in the summer of 2013 and has been battling it out with Bartosz Bialkowski for the number one spot at Portman Road.

02 JANOI **DONACIEN**

DEFENDER   DOB: 03/11/1993   COUNTRY: ST LUCIA

Donacien progressed through Aston Villa's Academy and has been a mainstay in the Accrington Stanley first team for the last two seasons. He joined the Blues in the summer of 2018 and can play anywhere across the back four.

03 JONAS **KNUDSEN**

DEFENDER   DOB: 16/09/1992   COUNTRY: DENMARK

Energetic Knudsen has been a regular fixture in the first team since he joined the Blues in 2015. He represented Denmark at the World Cup in Russia and caused havoc against Croatia with his signature long throws!

SQUAD 2018/19

05 MATTHEW **PENNINGTON**

DEFENDER DOB: 06/10/1994 COUNTRY: ENGLAND

A central defender, Pennington joined on a season-long loan from Premier League side Everton in August 2018. He spent the 2017/18 campaign on loan at Leeds United, where he made over 20 Championship appearances.

04 LUKE **CHAMBERS**

DEFENDER DOB: 28/09/1985 COUNTRY: ENGLAND

Central defender and club captain, Chambo has relished the challenge of impressing new manager, Paul Hurst this season. He is approaching 300 appearances for the Tractor Boys!

06 TREVOH **CHALOBAH**

DEFENDER DOB: 05/07/1999 COUNTRY: ENGLAND

Chalobah joined Town on a season-long loan from Chelsea in June 2018. At 18, Trevoh was an unused substitute for Chelsea as they won the FA Cup at Wembley with a 1-0 win over Manchester United. He is also capped for England at numerous youth levels.

08 COLE **SKUSE**

MIDFIELDER DOB: 29/03/1986 COUNTRY: ENGLAND

Skuse has been a constant in the team since he arrived at Portman Road as a free agent in the summer of 2013. He reached the impressive milestone of 200 appearances for Town last season and signed a new contract that will keep him a Blue until 2020 at least and he has said that he would be happy to finish his career at Town.

07 GWION **EDWARDS**

MIDFIELDER DOB: 01/03/1993 COUNTRY: WALES

Welsh winger Edwards joined Town in the summer of 2018 on a two-year deal from Peterborough United where he made over 50 appearances. He headed his debut goal at home against Blackburn Rovers on the opening day of the season.

09 KAYDEN **JACKSON**

FORWARD DOB: 22/02/1994 COUNTRY: ENGLAND

Jackson signed for the Blues from Accrington Stanley for an undisclosed fee in August 2018, signing a three-year deal. The striker played for Paul Hurst briefly at Grimsby, but joined up with the Blues boss again having scored 16 times in Stanley's push towards the League Two title in 2017/18.

11 JON **NOLAN**

MIDFIELDER **DOB:** 22/04/1992 **COUNTRY:** ENGLAND

Nolan joined the Blues from Shrewsbury Town in August 2018. He signed a three-year deal at Portman Road as he links up with Paul Hurst for the third time in his career, having already played for him at Grimsby and Shrewsbury.

10 ELLIS **HARRISON**

FORWARD **DOB:** 29/01/1994 **COUNTRY:** WALES

Harrison joined the Blues on a two-year deal from Bristol Rovers this summer. A former Wales U21 international, he bagged 14 times in all competitions for the Gas in the 2017/18 season, including a brace in a 6-0 win over Northampton. He also once scored four times in one game against the Cobblers in a 5-0 triumph in January 2017.

12 JORDAN **SPENCE**

DEFENDER **DOB:** 24/05/1990 **COUNTRY:** ENGLAND

Spence signed with the Blues in January 2017 and can either play at right-back or centre-back. He scored his first goal for the Club in August 2017, a late header from a free kick, that clinched a 4-3 victory over Millwall.

15 TEDDY **BISHOP**

MIDFIELDER **DOB: 15/07/1996** **COUNTRY: ENGLAND**

An Academy scholar who has progressed right through to the first team, since joining Town as an eight year-old. Bishop has been hindered by injury over the past three years but returned to action in the Carabao Cup clash at Exeter in August 2018, and Paul Hurst hopes he can make a big impact for Town this season.

14 JORDAN **GRAHAM**

MIDFIELDER **DOB: 05/03/1995** **COUNTRY: ENGLAND**

Graham joined on a season-long loan from Wolverhampton Wanderers in August 2018. He previously turned out for Blues in 2013 on a short loan from Aston Villa, making two substitute appearances.

17 DANNY **ROWE**

MIDFIELDER **DOB: 09/03/1992** **COUNTRY: ENGLAND**

Rowe joined Town on a three-and-a-half year deal in January 2017 from National League side Macclesfield Town. The wide-man damaged ankle ligaments at the back end of last season and has been focussed on building up his fitness.

18 GRANT **WARD**

MIDFIELDER   DOB: 05/12/1994   COUNTRY: ENGLAND

Grant joined the Blues in August 2016 from Tottenham and made an instant impact on his debut as he came off the bench at half-time in the 2016/17 season opener against Barnsley and scored within 39 seconds before soon adding a further two goals to complete a hat-trick.

19 JORDAN **ROBERTS**

MIDFIELDER   DOB: 05/01/1994   COUNTRY: ENGLAND

Roberts joined Town in June 2018 following his departure from Crawley Town. Prior to his spell with Crawley, Jordan spent time in Scotland with Inverness Caledonian Thistle. Jordan signed a two-year deal, keeping him under contract at Portman Road until 2020.

20 FREDDIE **SEARS**

FORWARD   DOB: 27/11/1989   COUNTRY: ENGLAND

Sears signed with the club back in January 2015 from Colchester United and has relished the opportunity to impress new boss, Paul Hurst. He started this season well, providing a perfect cross for Gwion Edwards to score Town's first goal of the season.

22 ARISTOTE NSIALA

DEFENDER **DOB: 25/03/1992** **COUNTRY: CONGO DR**

Central defender, Toto Nsiala signed for Town on a three-year deal from Shrewsbury in August 2018. It was the third time he had signed for Town boss Paul Hurst, having worked with him at both Salop and Grimsby in previous seasons.

21 FLYNN DOWNES

MIDFIELDER **DOB: 20/01/1999** **COUNTRY: ENGLAND**

Downes went on loan to League Two Luton Town for the second half of the 2017/18 season. He received glowing reports from their manager, Nathan Jones, and made a total of ten appearances for the Hatters as they were promoted to League One.

23 ANDRE DOZZELL

MIDFIELDER **DOB: 02/05/1999** **COUNTRY: ENGLAND**

A product of Town's academy, Dozzell made his debut at just 16 years old, scoring a header in a 1-1 draw with Sheffield Wednesday at Hillsborough. He played just 45 minutes of football last term due to a cruciate ligament injury suffered on the opening day of the campaign but has been working to be back on top form this season.

24 TOM **ADEYEMI**

MIDFIELDER **DOB: 24/10/1991** **COUNTRY: ENGLAND**

2017/18 was Adeyemi's debut season with Town. The former Canary spent the 2016/17 season on loan at Rotherham from Cardiff City where he scored seven times in all competitions. He has also had spells with Bradford, Oldham, Brentford and Leeds in his career so far.

25 ADETAYO **EDUN**

MIDFIELDER **DOB: 14/05/1998** **COUNTRY: ENGLAND**

Town signed Tayo Edun on a season-long loan from Fulham this summer. He made two appearances in the Championship for Play-Off winners Fulham last term, as well as lining up in the Carabao Cup. He has represented England at youth level up to U20 and was in the U19 squad that won the U19 European Championship last year.

27 JOSH **EMMANUEL**

DEFENDER **DOB: 18/08/1997** **COUNTRY: ENGLAND**

A strong right-back who signed with the Blues back in July 2015, Emmanuel joined Rotherham United on loan in 2017/18 and helped the Millers to promotion back to the Championship via the Play-Offs. He is currently on loan at Shrewsbury.

30 MYLES **KENLOCK**

DEFENDER   DOB: 26/11/1996   COUNTRY: ENGLAND

Kenlock joined the Blues in 2014 as a scholar, following trials at several clubs including some in the Premier League, as well as previously being on the books at Crystal Palace. He signed a new two-year deal in 2017.

32 LUKE **WOOLFENDEN**

DEFENDER   DOB: 21/10/1998   COUNTRY: ENGLAND

Woolfenden is an Academy graduate who progressed into the first-team squad and signed his first professional contract last season. He can play full-back or in the middle of the defence. He is currently on loan at Swindon.

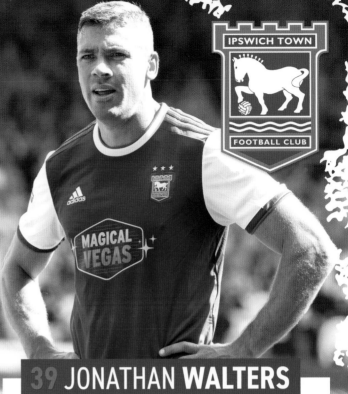

39 JONATHAN **WALTERS**

FORWARD **DOB:** 20/09/1983 **COUNTRY:** REPUBLIC OF IRELAND

Walters returned to Portman Road for his second spell in August 2018 as he joined on loan from Burnley until January. He first signed for Town over a decade ago in 2007 before leaving to join Stoke in 2010 having made well over 100 appearances for the Blues.

33 BARTOSZ **BIALKOWSKI**

GOALKEEPER **DOB:** 06/07/1987 **COUNTRY:** POLAND

Bialkowski joined the Blues back in July 2014 and has become a firm fans' favourite and this summer committed his future to Town by signing a new three year contract. He was voted Player of the Year by the supporters for the third successive time in 2017/18.

44 EMYR **HUWS**

MIDFIELDER **DOB:** 30/09/1993 **COUNTRY:** WALES

A box-to-box midfielder, Huws made his stay at Portman Road a permanent one in the summer of 2017 following a successful loan spell in the second half of the 16/17 campaign. He has also made several international appearances for Wales.

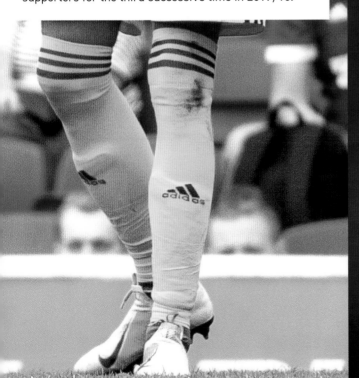

PRACTICE MAKES PERFECT

Practice, preparation and perseverance are all well-known key ingredients to success in the modern game. Long before the Blues run out at Portman Road, they will have gone through a thorough and detailed spell of work at the club's busy training centre.

The Blues' training ground is geared up to ensure that Paul Hurst's men are fully equipped for the Championship challenges that lie ahead. The modern-day player will not only be given the best of surfaces to practice on, but also given the very best advice and guidance in terms of their fitness, diet, rest and mental approach to performing at their maximum.

A typical day will begin with a series of physical tests, being weighed and taking part in a number of aerobic exercises, before blood levels and heart rates are measured.

Diet is vital to any player's wellbeing and performance levels, so a suitable breakfast is provided before the players head to the gymnasium to enjoy their own personal work-outs.

Prior to taking to the training pitches, players will be provided with a GPS tracking system and heart rate analysis monitors ensuring that all they do can be measured, monitored and reviewed. Then the physical conditioning begins out on the pitches. The manager and coaches will get down to working on various drills, set-piece situations and practice matches in the day's main session.

After a warm-down programme, it's off for a healthy lunch and a return to the gym for a strength, power and injury presentation session and feedback on the day's activities will be provided to the manager, coaches and players by the sports science department.

Come match day, this is where all the team's hard work and dedication through the week will make the difference.

7

GWION
EDWARDS

BORN:
21 DECEMBER 1953 · CANNOCK, STAFFORDSHIRE

POSITION:
GOALKEEPER

BLUES DEBUT:
LEEDS UNITED 3-2 IPSWICH TOWN · FIRST DIVISION · 20 APRIL 1974

ALL CLUBS:
BIRMINGHAM CITY, IPSWICH TOWN, LEICESTER CITY, MANCHESTER CITY, STOCKPORT COUNTY

PLAYER OF THE SEASON:
1980-81

BLUES APPEARANCES:

APPEARANCES	LEAGUE	CUPS
575	447	128

STAT ATTACK

PAUL COOPER

After making just 17 league appearances for Birmingham City, goalkeeper Paul Cooper joined Ipswich Town in 1974 and proceeded to become a legendary figure at Portman Road, playing 575 times for the club.

Cooper was an excellent all-round 'keeper with assured handling and great reflexes but it was his remarkable ability to save penalties that saw him become such a terrace hero. In the 1979/80 season he saved an incredible eight out of ten penalties.

A member of the 1978 FA Cup winning team and also a UEFA Cup winner in 1981, Cooper remains the Town 'keeper that all others will be judged against.

DANGER MEN

Watch out for these Danger Men when Town meet their Championship rivals...

ASTON VILLA
Jack Grealish

Attacking midfielder Jack Grealish is sure to be the driving force behind Aston Villa once again in 2018/19.

The talented playmaker is a Villa fan and will be going full throttle to help Steve Bruce's side win promotion back to the Premier League. Villa were delighted to keep him at the club following a summer of speculation about the England Under-21 star's future.

BOLTON WANDERERS
Yanic Wildschut

Dutch midfielder Yanic Wildschut joined Bolton Wanderers on a season-long loan deal from Championship rivals Norwich City in July 2018

The talented 27-year-old, who loves to run at the opposition, enjoyed the perfect start to his Bolton career by scoring the winning goal on the opening day of the season away to West Bromwich Albion

BIRMINGHAM CITY
Che Adams

After joining Blues from Sheffield United in August 2016, all-action midfielder Che Adams wasted little time in showing the St Andrew's faithful just what he was all about.

Adams wrote his name into Birmingham City folklore on the final day of the 2016/17 campaign, scoring the goal that preserved the club's Championship status. He is sure to be a key player for Garry Monk's men in 2018/19.

BRENTFORD
Ollie Watkins

One of the most exciting and talented footballers outside of the Premier League, Ollie Watkins has been a roaring success since joining Brentford from Exeter City in the summer of 2017.

He netted an impressive eleven goals in all competitions in his first season at Griffin Park. He loves to let fly from distance and has scored a number of spectacular goals for the Bees.

BLACKBURN ROVERS
Elliott Bennett

Experienced winger Elliott Bennett played a vital role in Rovers' promotion from League One in 2017/18.

The former Brighton and Norwich man has been a great influence on the younger players at Ewood Park and will be an important member of Tony Mowbray's team once again now they are back in the Championship.

BRISTOL CITY
Andreas Weimann

Much-travelled Austrian striker Andreas Weimann joined Bristol City ahead of the 2018/19 season, agreeing a three-year deal at Ashton Gate.

Weimann is a vastly experienced forward who knows the English game well following spells with Aston Villa, Watford, Derby County and Wolves. The Robins will be looking for Weimann to grab the goals to fire them into Play-Off contention.

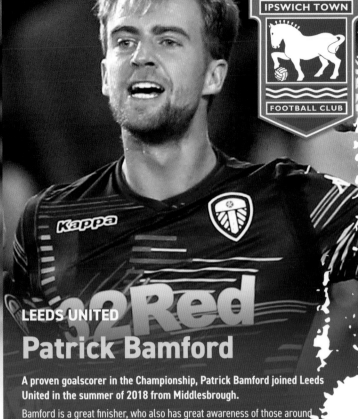

DERBY COUNTY
Tom Lawrence

Wales international midfielder Tom Lawrence, looks set to play a vital role at Pride Park in 2018/19 under new Derby boss Frank Lampard.

The Rams' midfielder certainly has an eye for goal and with Lampard to guide him, Lawrence could well become one of the Championship's star turns over the coming months. He began the season in fine form with two goals in Derby's opening two games.

LEEDS UNITED
Patrick Bamford

A proven goalscorer in the Championship, Patrick Bamford joined Leeds United in the summer of 2018 from Middlesbrough.

Bamford is a great finisher, who also has great awareness of those around him. His arrival at Elland Road has certainly heightened the levels of expectation among the Leeds United fans.

HULL CITY
Fraizer Campbell

Vastly-experienced striker Fraizer Campbell brings an enormous amount of know-how to the Tigers' front line.

A former England international, Campbell has spent time on the books at some of the country's biggest clubs including Manchester United and Tottenham Hotspur. Now in his second spell with Hull, he was on target against Sheffield Wednesday to ensure the Tigers' first point of the 2018/19 season.

MIDDLESBROUGH
Britt Assombalonga

Former Nottingham Forest striker Britt Assombalonga joined Middlesbrough in July 2015 for a club record fee of £15M.

He was a consistent goalscorer with both Peterborough United and Forest. Assombalonga netted 13 goals as Boro reached the Play-Off semi-finals last season. Boro will be looking for him to be heavily among the goals again in 2018/19 as they look to mount a successful promotion bid.

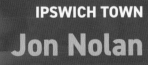

IPSWICH TOWN
Jon Nolan

Talented midfielder Jon Nolan was an instrumental player for Shrewsbury Town in 2017/18 as the Shrews reached both the Checkatrade Trophy final and the League One Play-Off final.

In August 2018, he joined Ipswich Town and reunited with his former Shrewsbury boss Paul Hurst who took over at Portman Road three months earlier. Nolan is expected to flourish at Championship level.

MILLWALL
Steve Morison

Evergreen forward Steve Morison is currently enjoying his second spell with the Lions.

His goals helped propel the South London club to the verge of the Play-Offs last season. Approaching 300 games for Millwall and almost 100 goals, Morison is a vital member of Neil Harris' squad with a positive influence both on and off the pitch.

DANGER MEN

Watch out for these Danger Men when Town meet their Championship rivals…

NORWICH CITY
Jordan Rhodes

Signed on loan from Sheffield Wednesday, the Canaries will be hopeful that striker Jordan Rhodes can rediscover his goalscoring form during the 2018/19 season at Carrow Road.

A prolific marksman with Huddersfield Town and Blackburn Rovers, Rhodes marked his Carrow Road debut with a goal during a thrilling seven goal clash with West Bromwich Albion.

QUEENS PARK RANGERS
Conor Washington

Northern Ireland international striker Conor Washington made his name in the lower divisions with impressive scoring spells for Newport County and Peterborough United.

He joined Rangers in January 2016 and his all-action displays soon made him a favourite with the Loftus Road crowd. Washington will be keen to impress under former England boss Steve McClaren this season.

NOTTINGHAM FOREST
Lewis Grabban

A proven Championship goalscorer, Lewis Grabban joined Nottingham Forest in July 2018 for a fee believed to have been in the region of £6M.

His arrival at the City Ground is expected to relieve some of the pressure for goals on fellow frontman Daryl Murphy. Grabban has played for a host of clubs and appears to have the handy knack of always taking his scoring boots with him.

READING
Jon Dadi Bodvarsson

Icelandic international forward Jon Dadi Bodvarsson has become something of a cult hero with Reading fans at the Madejski Stadium after netting ten goals for the Royals last season.

He represented his country at the 2018 World Cup finals in Russia and also netted Reading's first goal of the new 2018/19 campaign.

PRESTON NORTH END
Tom Barkhuizen

After beginning his career with Preston's rivals Blackpool, striker Tom Barkhuizen is a player who will be looking to make his mark for Alex Neil's side in 2018/19.

A string of loan spells with Hereford United, Fleetwood Town and Morecambe resulted in a permanent switch to Morecambe and it was his goalscoring form at the Globe Arena that alerted North End who signed him in November 2016.

ROTHERHAM UNITED
Joe Newell

Versatile midfielder Joe Newell was one of the Millers' heroes as Rotherham United won promotion to the Championship via the League One Play-Offs.

With the ability to operate in a creative central midfield berth or out on the wing, Newell was almost ever-present for the Millers last season and will be a key performer for Paul Warne's men in their 2018/19 Championship campaign.

22

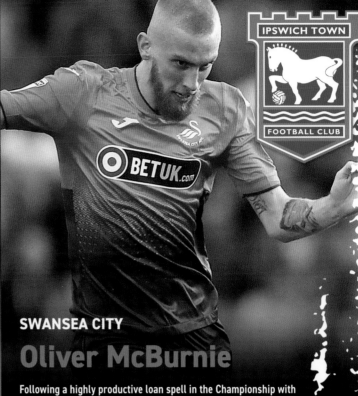

SHEFFIELD UNITED
Billy Sharp

Now in his third spell with the Blades, and still looking as lively as ever in front of goal, Billy Sharp will once again be at the forefront of manager Chris Wilder's thoughts at Bramall Lane

Sharp became the Sheffield United captain in 2016 and is now closing in on 200 goals for the club.

SWANSEA CITY
Oliver McBurnie

Following a highly productive loan spell in the Championship with Barnsley in the second half of last season, Oliver McBurnie has earned the chance to lead the line for Swansea City as the Welsh club bid to bounce back to the top flight in 2018/19.

McBurnie scored nine goals in 17 outings for a struggling Tykes team last season and will now look to grab his Swansea opportunity with both hands.

SHEFFIELD WEDNESDAY
Fernando Forestieri

The jewel in Sheffield Wednesday's crown, all eyes at Hillsborough will once again be on skilful Italian Fernando Forestieri who is the man that makes the Owls tick.

The Wednesday fans will be looking for Forestieri to inspire those around him as the club searches for an improved season under Jos Luhakay.

WEST BROMWICH ALBION
Jay Rodriguez

Burnley-born England striker Jay Rodriguez began his career at his hometown club before moving on to the Premier League with Southampton and then West Bromwich Albion.

A cool customer with the ball at his feet, Rodriguez has all the skills to really shine in the Championship for an Albion side who will hope their stay in the second tier is a brief one.

STOKE CITY
Benik Afobe

Striker Benik Afobe is the man charged with scoring the goals to fire Stoke City back to the Premier League at the first time of asking.

Afobe joined the Potters on loan from Wolverhampton Wanderers in June 2018 and his physical presence and goal threat are sure to play a huge part in the Potters' 2018/19 promotion push.

WIGAN ATHLETIC
Nick Powell

Midfielder Nick Powell was nominated for the EFL League One Player of the Season award after an outstanding season in the Latics 2017/18 title-winning campaign.

A technically gifted player with the ability to score goals and create chances for others, Powell will certainly be one of the first names on Paul Cook's teamsheet as Wigan look to establish themselves at Championship level.

Magic MOMENT 77'

WE'VE WON THE Cup

FIXTURE: FA Cup final

DATE: Saturday, 6 May 1978

SCORE: Ipswich Town 1 Arsenal 0

VENUE: Wembley Stadium

ATTENDANCE: 100,000

Roger Osborne cemented his name in Ipswich Town history as he netted the only goal of the game to ensure Town lifted the FA Cup at Wembley in 1978.

Under the management of Bobby Robson, Town had dominated the showpiece final against Arsenal and had hit the woodwork on three occasions before Osborne's 77th minute moment of glory.

Clive Woods and David Geddis combined to set up Osborne who scored with a left-foot shot. In the aftermath of the goal celebrations, Osborne actually fainted before having to be substituted. Despite Osborne's late withdrawal, his work was done, and the cup was coming to Suffolk.

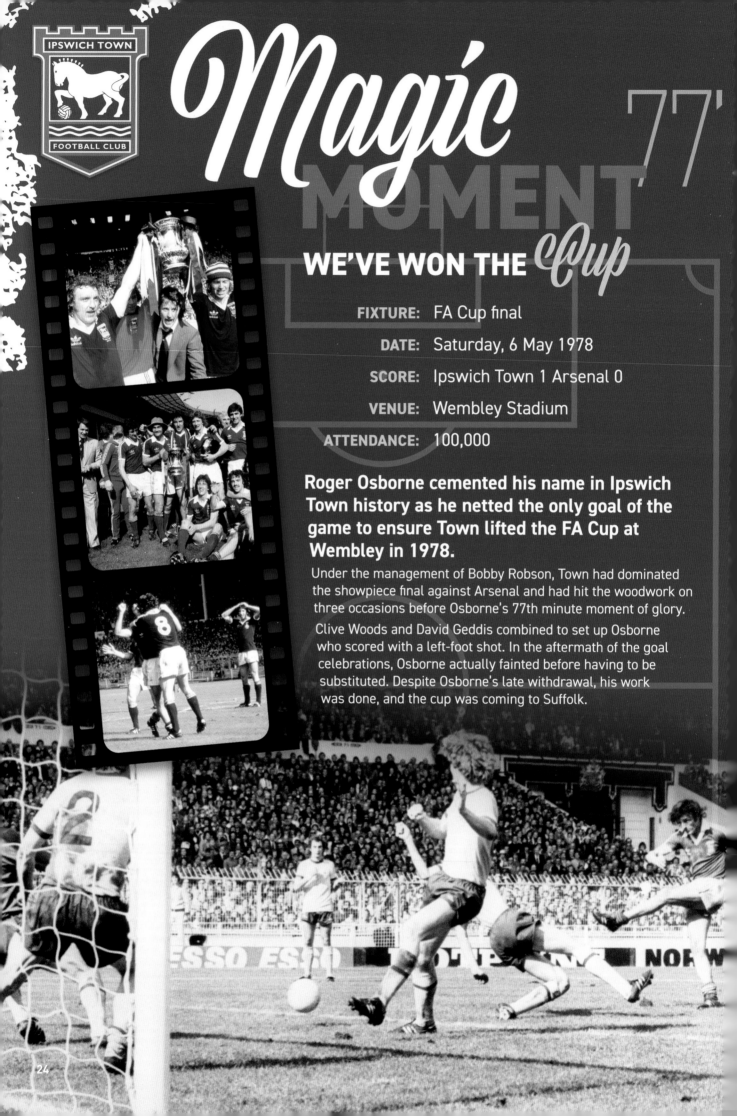

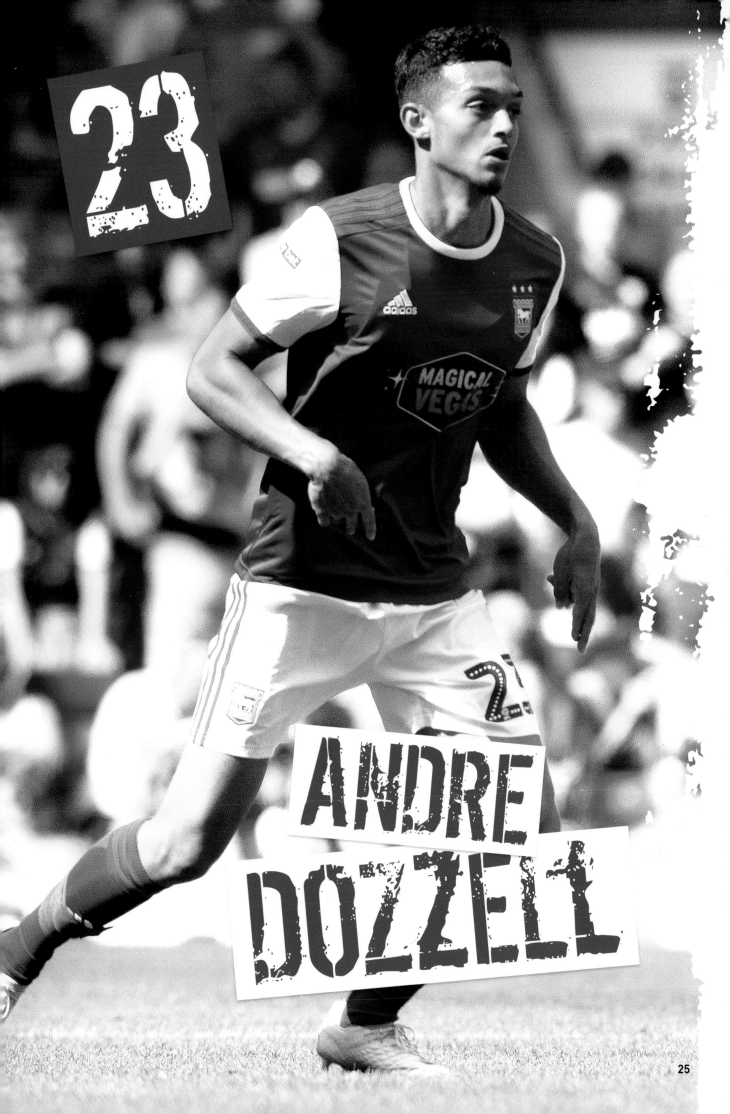

23

ANDRE DOZZELL

ANSWERS ON PAGE 62

There are five England World Cup stars hiding in the crowd... can you find them all?

27

#BOYSGOTSKILLS
THE PUSKAS MOVE

Ferenc Puskas is one of the greatest footballers of all time and the creator of the famous 'V' move that you can see used in most games of football. It allows you to change direction quickly and fool your defender. The move is very simple but hard to master at speed.

TIP:
Use this move when you need to lose your defender. Pretend to strike the ball, your opponent will move to block your faked shot, allowing you to move freely in another direction.

TIP:
Always wait until your defender lunges for the ball before performing the Puskas move.

1. Start by dribbling the ball, keep it as near to your foot as possible while moving forward.

2. Move as if to kick the ball, but rather than striking it, bring your foot over the top of the ball.

TIP:
Don't perform this move too often or your opponents will learn to expect it!

3. Use the bottom of your foot to quickly drag the ball back to you.

4. Now change direction. You can finish the move with a shot at goal or by passing to a teammate.

10 ELLIS HARRISON

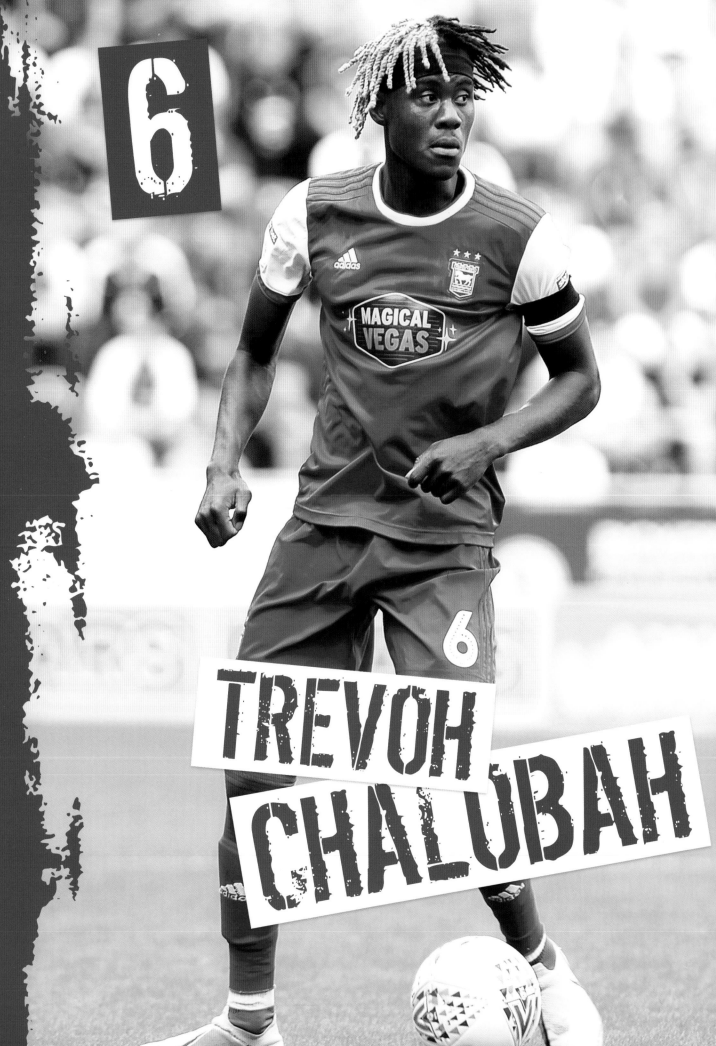

6

TREVOH CHALOBAH

BORN:

4 AUGUST 1957 · GLASGOW

POSITION:

MIDFIELDER

BLUES DEBUT:

IPSWICH TOWN 3-2 LEEDS UNITED
FA CUP · 27 MARCH 1975

ALL CLUBS:

IPSWICH TOWN, LIVERPOOL, IPSWICH TOWN,
MIDDLESBROUGH, IPSWICH TOWN

BLUES PLAYER OF THE SEASON:

1988/89, 1989/90, 1991/92 & 1994/94

BLUES APPEARANCES:

APPEARANCES	LEAGUE	CUPS
678	539	139

BLUES GOALS:

GOALS	LEAGUE	CUPS
179	135	44

STAT ATTACK

JOHN WARK

SCOTLAND INTERNATIONAL:

APPEARANCES	GOALS
29	7

INTERNATIONAL DEBUT:

19 MAY 1979 · WALES 3-0 SCOTLAND

Town legend John Wark amassed a total of 678 appearances for the Blues, 670 starts and eight substitute appearances, over three separate spells at Portman Road.

Born is Glasgow, Wark was a goalscoring midfielder who progressed through the youth and reserve ranks to become a real star performer during the club's golden era under Bobby Robson.

A member of Town's 1978 FA Cup winning team, Wark's goals were the catalyst for the club's UEFA Cup triumph in 1981. He scored 14 goals in the competition including one in each leg of the final as Town overcame Dutch side AZ Alkmaar 5-4 on aggregate.

31

BART'S HAT-TRICK

Bartosz Bialkowski was named Supporters' Player of the Year for the third successive season last term. The Polish goalkeeper enjoyed another inspirational campaign in the Town net, pulling off a number of breathtaking saves to ensure an end of season highlight reel to be proud of!

The Blues shot-stopper tweeted after winning the award:

> "It's an absolute honour to have won Player of the Season three times in a row! I would like to thank every single one of you."

The Pole's form throughout the campaign not only earned recognition from the Blue Army, but also on the international stage. His performances for Town ensured he won his first cap for his country, before taking his place in Poland's squad for the World Cup in Russia.

Following his return from Russia, and to the delight of Town fans, the Blues custodian signed a new contract with the club. After penning the deal he tweeted a message to his loyal supporters: 'It's a great honour to play for this great football club.'

Only John Wark has won the award more times for Town than the 'keeper, doing so on four occasions.

Can Bart make it four wins in a row in 2019?

PLAYER OF THE SEASON

BARTOSZ BIALKOWSKI

GOAL OF THE SEASON

Bersant Celina added some flair to the Town midfield during the 2017/18 campaign. The Manchester City loanee scored a number of stunning goals with the pick of the bunch coming in January against Leeds United at Portman Road.

After picking the ball up from a throw in mid-way inside the Leeds half, the midfielder skipped past two defenders before unleashing a thunderous effort from 30 yards. The ball flew past opposing 'keeper Felix Wiedwald and into the top corner of the net.

After an acrobatic fly kick to an unsuspecting corner flag Celina ran over to celebrate the memorable effort with the ecstatic home fans. The second-half stunner proved to be the winner with the Kosovan international securing a valuable three points in front of the Blue Army.

BERSANT CELINA V LEEDS

33

GUESS THE CLUB

Can you work out which European club each set of clues is pointing to?

1 ANSWER

3 ANSWER

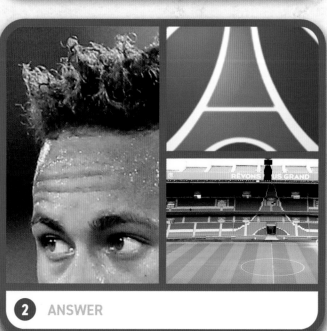

2 ANSWER

4 ANSWER

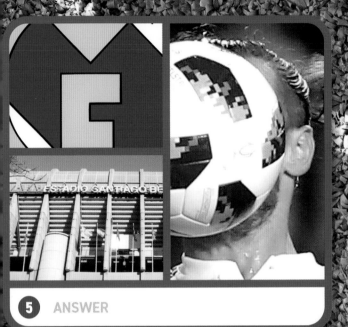

5 ANSWER

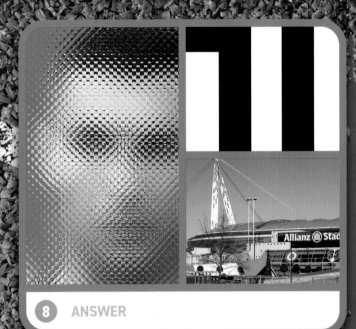

8 ANSWER

6 ANSWER

9 ANSWER

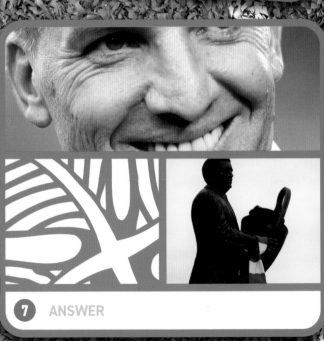

7 ANSWER

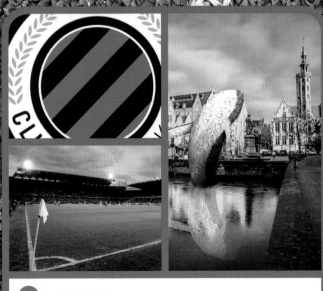

10 ANSWER

LOCAL HEROES

ALEX MATHIE

IAN MARSHALL

TOWN 5 NORWICH 0
DESTRUCTION DERBY
21 FEBRUARY 1998

Town put five past Norwich at Portman Road with Bobby Petta scoring a brace and Alex Mathie delivering a first-half hat-trick. Former captain Matt Holland and Mathie both went on to describe the game as their most memorable East Anglian derby, with Mathie revealing:

"Someone came to my house and gave me a bottle of whisky and said, 'thanks for making me happy for the next six months'. That is what winning the derby means to the fans."

TOWN 2 NORWICH 1
DERBY DIVOT
14 APRIL 1996

This Derby looked to be fizzling out for a 1-1 draw until the 86th minute, when what seemed to be an innocent backpass from Rob Ullathorne ended up going down in Ipswich folklore.

Town had taken the lead through Ian Marshall, before Jamie Cureton replied for the visitors, then the Portman Road pitch took centre stage. Ullathorne rolled an innocuous pass to his 'keeper Bryan Gunn, who attempted a first-time clearance. Enter the 'derby divot' and the rest is history as they say!

NORWICH 1 TOWN 2
THE CANARY CRUSHER
5 FEBRUARY 2006

Town bagged all three points in this East Anglian derby courtesy of a controversial winner from Danny Haynes, although it was later ruled a Gary Doherty own goal. Haynes bundled the ball over the line with just two minutes remaining to seal victory for Joe Royle's side at Carrow Road.

Jonatan Johansson chipped Town 'keeper Lewis Price for the opener on 33 minutes but the Blues equalised immediately through Jimmy Juan. Both sides searched for a winner, but it was Haynes on hand in the dying stages to snatch victory for the Blues. Overall Haynes scored four goals in five senior games against Norwich.

TOWN 3 NORWICH 2
MEXICAN RAVE
19 APRIL 2009

Town's victory proved to last longer than 90 minutes as the three points played a pivotal role in condemning Norwich to relegation to League One. Mexican international Giovanni Dos Santos, on loan from Tottenham, led the Canaries a merry dance and proved to be the inspiration behind Town's win.

Alan Quinn and then a Gio penalty put Town in front after David Mooney had headed the Canaries into the lead. Jon Stead calmly slotted into the bottom corner for what seemed to be a decisive third strike for Town, but Sammy Clingan found the net from the spot to create a nervy finale. The Blues held on to take the spoils though and pushed Norwich towards the trapdoor.

37

Magic
MOMENT

90'

GOING Up

FIXTURE:	First Division Play-Off final
DATE:	Monday, 29 May 2000
SCORE:	Ipswich Town 4 Barnsley 2
VENUE:	Wembley Stadium
ATTENDANCE:	73,427

After so many play-off heartbreaks, Town finally secured promotion to the Premier League via the end-of-season lottery, as they defeated Barnsley at Wembley in 2000.

In a highly eventful and topsy-turvy match, that had seen Town trail 1-0, lead 3-1, they headed into the closing minutes with a slender 3-2 advantage.

Martijn Reuser became the toast of Suffolk as the Dutchman was set free by Richard Naylor and smashed home a 90th minute goal to put all doubts to bed and seal Town's promotion.

4

LUKE
CHAMBERS

Can you
identify all of
these Town stars?

1

2

3

4

5

40

6

7

8

WHO ARE YER?

9

10

MAGICAL VEGAS

41

IPSWICH TOWN
FOOTBALL CLUB

11

MAGICAL VEGAS

JON NOLAN

#BOYSGOTSKILLS
THE FLIP FLAP

Practise! Practise! Practise!

1. Start by getting familiar with the leg movement.

Push the ball with the outside of your foot.

TIP: Try performing the movement while hopping

TIP: Practise performing the movement while moving forwards and backwards

2. Then move your foot around the ball and bring it back in towards your body.

AKA 'the Elastico'

This move is used by many players and was made famous first by Rivelino in the 1970s and more recently by Ronaldinho. It is a simple technique and done right, really works! The idea behind it is to unbalance your defender by moving the ball one way before using some tricky footwork to move off in another direction!

3. Once you're familiar with the movement, try it while dribbling the ball forward.

TIP: Work on perfecting the technique, then when you're ready you can start moving the ball further away from your body to really confuse your defender

4. Push the ball with the outside of your foot, away from your body. As your defender moves in the direction of the ball...

5. ...Move your foot around the ball, drag it back across your body and move off in the other direction.

43

We take a look
at three great
Blues games
from last season...

<<REWIND

MILLWALL 3-4 TOWN
15 AUGUST 2017

Jordan Spence was the man of the moment as Town maintained a 100% winning start to the season with an incredible victory at Millwall in August.

The Den played host to a Championship classic as the two sides combined for seven goals, with Mick McCarthy's men heading home with all three points. Blues couldn't have got off to a worse start, though, as Jed Wallace volleyed Millwall ahead after just 44 seconds. Joe Garner responded for Town before Martyn Waghorn smashed the visitors ahead, and made it 3-2 after Aiden O'Brien had equalised. Millwall thought they had nicked a point through Tom Elliott's strike, but Blues' Spence rose highest to nod in a dramatic winner in the final moments.

TOWN 4-2 NOTTINGHAM FOREST
2 DECEMBER 2017

Town prevailed in a six-goal thriller against Nottingham Forest at Portman Road back in December. Blues' Callum Connolly opened the scoring just seven minutes in but the visitors replied through Kieran Dowell's free-kick on the half-hour mark.

Dominic Iorfa restored Town's advantage with a towering header eight minutes before the break but once again Forest levelled as Tyler Walker found the back of the net. Martyn Waghorn put Blues ahead for a third time in the 53rd minute with a cool finish before teeing up Bersant Celina to wrap up all three points for the hosts just after the hour mark.

NORWICH 1-1 TOWN
18 FEBRUARY 2018

Blues were seconds away from a first win over their bitter East Anglian rivals at Carrow Road in February. Canaries shot-stopper Angus Gunn and Blues 'keeper Bartosz Bialkowski were both called into action in what was a tense encounter.

The game truly kicked into life, though, in the 89th minute. Town skipper Luke Chambers beautifully met a Martyn Waghorn corner as the Blues thought they had snatched victory in the final moments. But, deep into five minutes of stoppage time, it was heartbreak for the travelling Blue Army as Norwich defender Timm Klose headed home to share the spoils.

1

Who scored Town's first league goal last season?

ANSWER

2

Which player joined Town from Nottingham Forest on transfer deadline day, January 2018?

ANSWER

3

Who made the most league appearances for the Blues last season?

ANSWER

4

Last season, Town's highest goalscoring performance was against which team and what was the score?

ANSWER

5

How many points did the Tractor Boys finish the season with in 2017/18?

ANSWER

6

What was the score when the Blues knocked Luton Town out of the first round of the EFL Cup in August 2017?

ANSWER

2017/18 END OF TERM EXAM

How much did you learn about the Blues' last campaign?

7

Who was Ipswich Town's first win against last season?

ANSWER

8

Who received the most yellow cards for the Blues last season?

ANSWER

9

Who top scored last season with 16 league goals?

ANSWER

10

How many clean sheets did Ipswich Town keep in the league last season?

ANSWER

ANSWERS ON PAGE 62

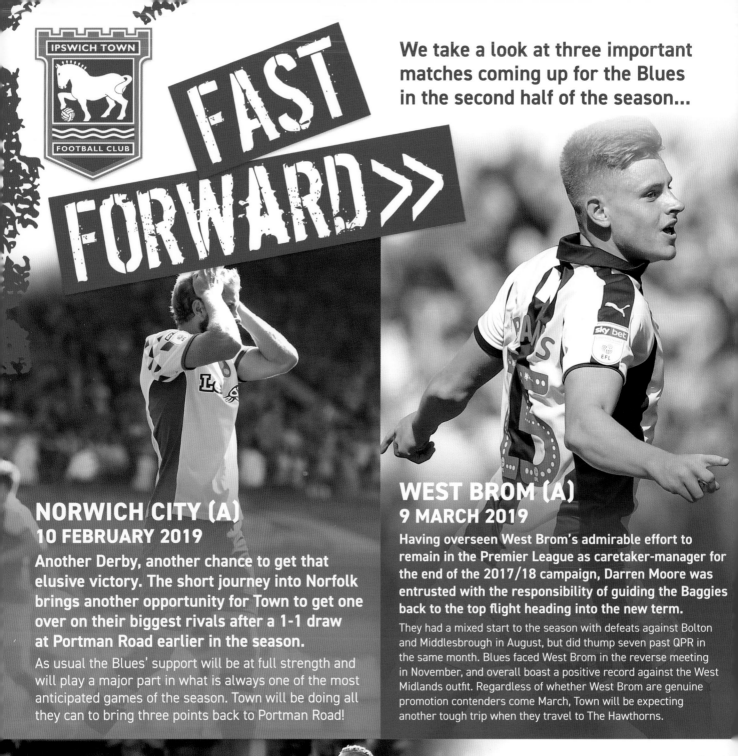

FAST FORWARD >>

We take a look at three important matches coming up for the Blues in the second half of the season...

NORWICH CITY (A)
10 FEBRUARY 2019

Another Derby, another chance to get that elusive victory. The short journey into Norfolk brings another opportunity for Town to get one over on their biggest rivals after a 1-1 draw at Portman Road earlier in the season.

As usual the Blues' support will be at full strength and will play a major part in what is always one of the most anticipated games of the season. Town will be doing all they can to bring three points back to Portman Road!

WEST BROM (A)
9 MARCH 2019

Having overseen West Brom's admirable effort to remain in the Premier League as caretaker-manager for the end of the 2017/18 campaign, Darren Moore was entrusted with the responsibility of guiding the Baggies back to the top flight heading into the new term.

They had a mixed start to the season with defeats against Bolton and Middlesbrough in August, but did thump seven past QPR in the same month. Blues faced West Brom in the reverse meeting in November, and overall boast a positive record against the West Midlands outfit. Regardless of whether West Brom are genuine promotion contenders come March, Town will be expecting another tough trip when they travel to The Hawthorns.

LEEDS UNITED (H)
5 MAY 2019

Leeds made a strong start to the season and by the start of September were top of the Championship table. Whether or not that form continues over the entirety of the season, Town will still be expecting a tough game at Portman Road come the start of May.

If there's something to play for in the final game for either team there is sure to be a vocal and passionate atmosphere at Portman Road with both sets of fans hoping to give their team the edge.

PREDICTION FOR PREMIER LEAGUE WINNERS:
Liverpool

YOUR
PREDICTION:

PREDICTION FOR CHAMPIONSHIP WINNERS:
Ipswich Town

YOUR
PREDICTION:

PREDICTION FOR FA CUP WINNERS:
Brighton & Hove Albion

YOUR
PREDICTION:

PREDICTION FOR PREMIER LEAGUE RUNNERS-UP:
Manchester City

YOUR
PREDICTION:

PREDICTION FOR CHAMPIONSHIP RUNNERS-UP:
Derby County

YOUR
PREDICTION:

2018/19 PREDICTIONS

Here are our predictions for the 2018/19 season.

What do you think will happen?

PREDICTION FOR PREMIER LEAGUE TOP SCORER:
Harry Kane

YOUR
PREDICTION:

PREDICTION FOR CHAMPIONSHIP TOP SCORER:
Kayden Jackson

YOUR
PREDICTION:

PREDICTION FOR LEAGUE CUP WINNERS:
Burnley

YOUR
PREDICTION:

47

#BOYSGOTSKILLS
THE OKOCHA STEP OVER

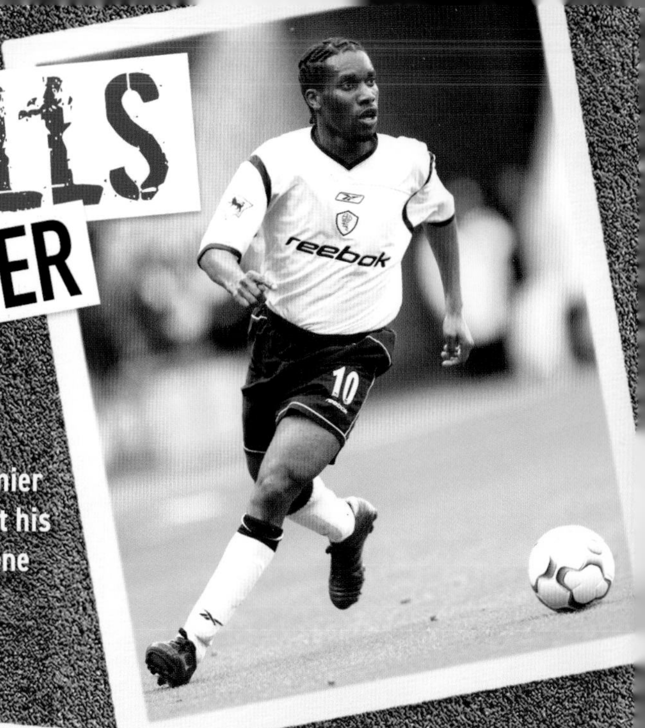

Jay-Jay Okocha was one of the best tricksters the Premier League has ever seen. He was effortless in getting past his opponents and here we take a look at how to perform one of his most famous moves...

1. While running...

...roll the ball with the inside of your right foot across your body to the left.

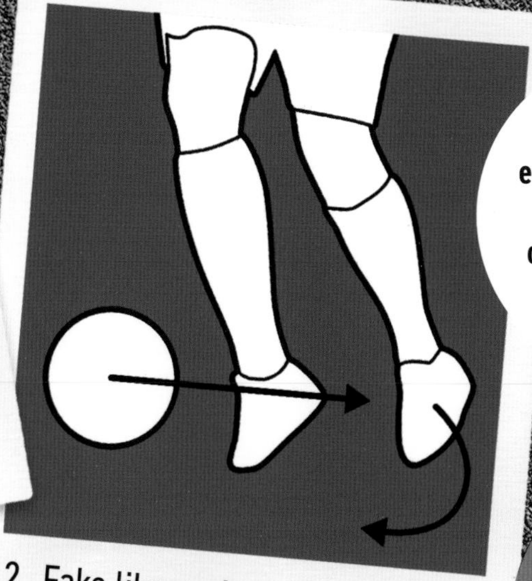

2. Fake like you're going to hit it with your left foot...

TIP:
Roll the ball far enough out across your body so it doesn't get stuck under your feet.

Tip:
Practise until you can master the move off both feet!

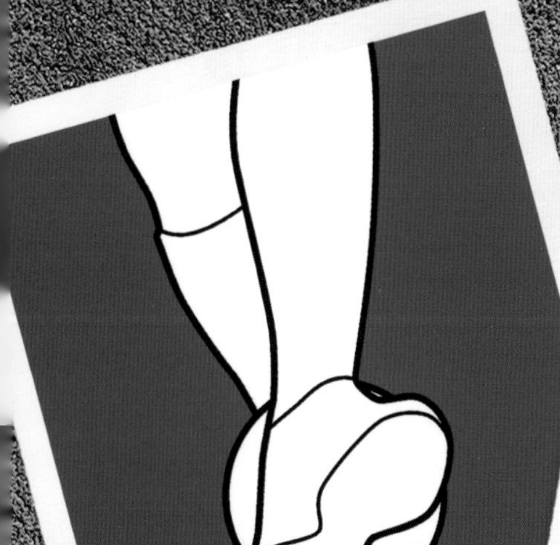

3. ...but step over it instead!

4. While you're performing the step over...

...do a quick body feint to the right to help throw off your opponent.

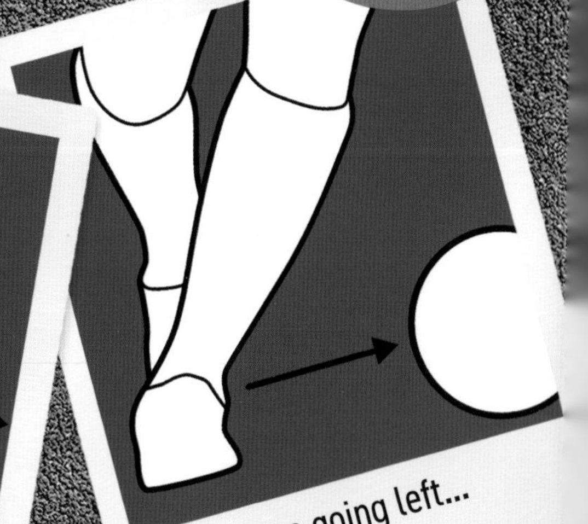

5. Continue going left...

...leaving your opponent wondering what just happened

3

IPSWICH TOWN
FOOTBALL CLUB

JONAS
KNUDSEN

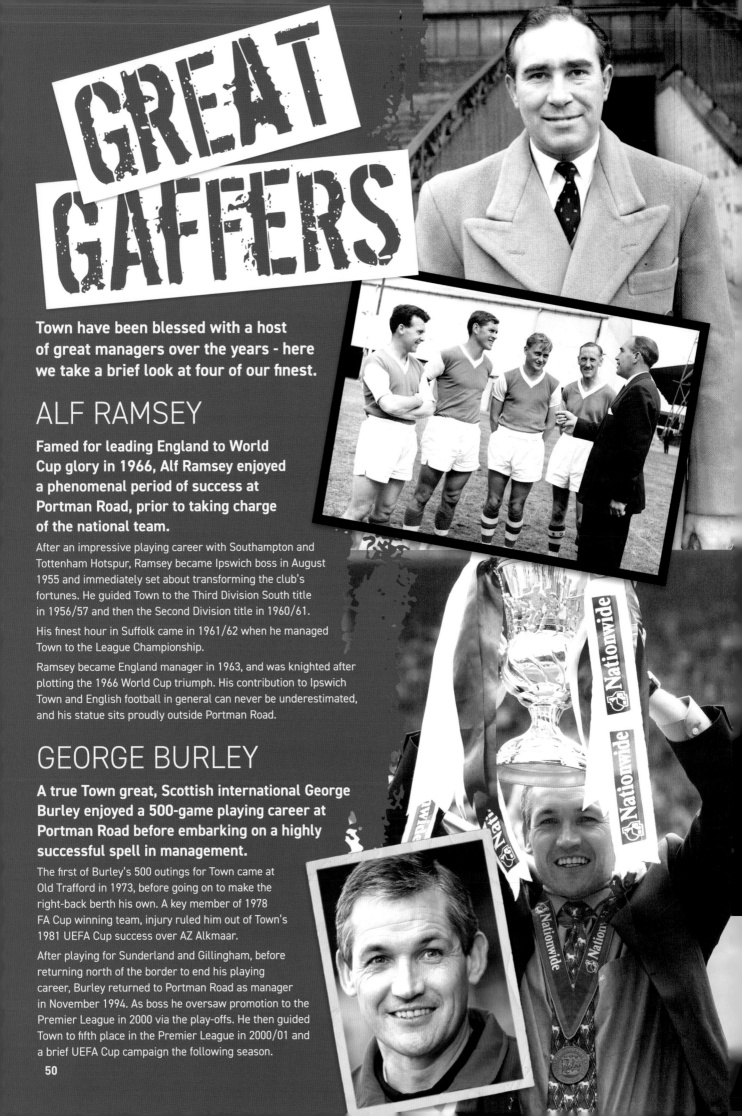

GREAT GAFFERS

Town have been blessed with a host of great managers over the years - here we take a brief look at four of our finest.

ALF RAMSEY

Famed for leading England to World Cup glory in 1966, Alf Ramsey enjoyed a phenomenal period of success at Portman Road, prior to taking charge of the national team.

After an impressive playing career with Southampton and Tottenham Hotspur, Ramsey became Ipswich boss in August 1955 and immediately set about transforming the club's fortunes. He guided Town to the Third Division South title in 1956/57 and then the Second Division title in 1960/61.

His finest hour in Suffolk came in 1961/62 when he managed Town to the League Championship.

Ramsey became England manager in 1963, and was knighted after plotting the 1966 World Cup triumph. His contribution to Ipswich Town and English football in general can never be underestimated, and his statue sits proudly outside Portman Road.

GEORGE BURLEY

A true Town great, Scottish international George Burley enjoyed a 500-game playing career at Portman Road before embarking on a highly successful spell in management.

The first of Burley's 500 outings for Town came at Old Trafford in 1973, before going on to make the right-back berth his own. A key member of 1978 FA Cup winning team, injury ruled him out of Town's 1981 UEFA Cup success over AZ Alkmaar.

After playing for Sunderland and Gillingham, before returning north of the border to end his playing career, Burley returned to Portman Road as manager in November 1994. As boss he oversaw promotion to the Premier League in 2000 via the play-offs. He then guided Town to fifth place in the Premier League in 2000/01 and a brief UEFA Cup campaign the following season.

JOHN LYALL

Always associated with West Ham United where he played and managed, John Lyall also tasted success as Town boss later in his managerial career.

Lyall succeeded John Duncan as Ipswich manager in 1990 and led the club to the Second Division title in 1991/92. That promotion ensured that Ipswich Town took their place among English football's elite as the Premier League era began in 1992/93.

Under Lyall's knowledgeable guidance, Town made an impressive start to the inaugural Premier League season and enjoyed a league double over arch-rivals Norwich City.

After ensuring Town's Premier League status again in 1993/94, Lyall became the club's Director of Football in the summer of 1994 with Mick McGiven taking responsibility of the first team on a day-to-day basis.

BOBBY ROBSON

Having previously managed Fulham, Bobby Robson was appointed Ipswich boss in January 1969, and led the club to a golden era during the late 1970s and early 80s.

Under Robson's guidance Town sampled FA Cup glory at Wembley in 1978 and were also League Championship runners-up in both 1980/81 and 1981/82.

The club also conquered Europe under Robson's management when they defeated AZ Alkmaar in the 1980/81 UEFA Cup final. During his lengthy spell in charge at Portman Road, Robson made a host of quality signings including Dutch superstars Frans Thijssen and Arnold Muhren.

In July 1982 Robson was named England manager and led the country to the World Cup semi-finals at Italia '90.

51

FIRST ELEVEN

Choose your all-time First Eleven, put their names and numbers on the back of the shirts, then colour them in!

IPSWICH TOWN FOOTBALL CLUB

SPOT THE BALL

The ball is missing from this photo, where should it be?

WHAT BALL?

Can you figure out which is the real ball in this photo?

JORDAN SPENCE

12

BORN:
11 APRIL 1974 · BURY, LANCASHIRE

POSITION:
MIDFIELDER

BLUES DEBUT:
QPR 0-0 IPSWICH TOWN
NATIONWIDE DIVISION ONE · 9 AUGUST 1997

ALL CLUBS:
AFC BOURNEMOUTH, IPSWICH TOWN, CHARLTON ATHLETIC

BLUES PLAYER OF THE SEASON:
1997/98 & 2002/03

BLUES APPEARANCES:

APPEARANCES	LEAGUE	FA CUP	LEAGUE CUP	OTHER
320	259	12	24	26

BLUES GOALS:

GOALS	LEAGUE	LEAGUE CUP	OTHER
48	38	6	4

STAT ATTACK
MATT HOLLAND

REPUBLIC OF IRELAND INTERNATIONAL:

APPEARANCES	GOALS
49	5

INTERNATIONAL DEBUT:
9 OCTOBER 1999 · MACEDONIA 1-1 REPUBLIC OF IRELAND

Recruited from AFC Bournemouth in the summer of 1997, for a fee of £800,000 - midfielder Matt Holland became a firm crowd favourite over the six years that he was an Ipswich player. His commitment and consistency won him many admirers and he was soon installed as captain.

In 1999/2000 Holland skippered Town to promotion following the Wembley Play-Off final victory over Barnsley. He starred in the Premier League in 2000/01 as Town finished fifth and represented the Republic of Ireland at the 2002 World Cup finals.

Remarkably, Holland missed just one league game for Town during his Portman Road career.

Here is a list of 20
Blues heroes. All but
one of their surnames are hidden
in the grid, can you work out who is missing?

I ♥ ITFC

```
B Z S T O K I V M D F V I R O E T J S H S A
A C U F L C U W E F H O C R A W F O R D Z H
L A I X N W Q S B V A Y G X E P M U Y V U K
A M L H U B P B B R U X M Y K H L I E Q C I
Z J D I A E D R A R G O I G W T C K T P U I
M H J Q B E A T T I E H D J A B F T H U D Q
B I C K M Z L R S E Z Z G B U N X I U C S F
G W L G I T V C G D M I D P J O L E N B M Z
V M K L T M E Y D A O U O W E L N X T T E A
P T N C S G O F R Y T E B Z I S B G E L V R
V I V R D U E I A F L E N P U E L W R T J T
F C E B L T N R F I Q H S G C M A K B C R G
M S D I H E V D C K M K X G H O L L A N D G
B U I W R R X I A J B R P Z O N Q Y O E K F
N E J N Q P Q S B N Y A E O H P O B P R E H
E O I C A E Z K O E Z M S L N T S I O H V F
S A S F D G Z N S O R Y E L R U B V J U G E
S O Y B S X E M W M B H O V G F O Q I M J I
J C L Z O K A S U Y L W H T A T R S E V Z M
I M U M M R F I R E U S E B N R N C K S L L
H R C I U N J R X T T X B H R W E J A D Q F
T I T B T O P D Q U R O D H F R U G A I E P
A S A J H I D O Z Z E L L Z W C X O A W A R
W U C B Y Q K S K V S O Z M U F P U O L N B
J T N V T P L A R U T Y M B M Q S B K R A W
```

Kevin **Beattie**	Jason **Dozzell**	Mick **Mills**	Alf **Ramsey**
Alan **Brazil**	Eric **Gates**	Arnold **Muhren**	Bobby **Robson**
George **Burley**	Matt **Holland**	Roger **Osborne**	Frans **Thijssen**
Terry **Butcher**	Allan **Hunter**	Russell **Osman**	John **Wark**
Ray **Crawford**	Paul **Mariner**	Ted **Phillips**	Trevor **Whymark**

ANSWERS ON PAGE 62

SHIRT SHUFFLE

1 RLVOELPOI

2 ALUMHF

3 FEEHFLDIS NIEUDT

4 RNGBIHMMIA TIYC

5 TEWS AMH DUTNIE

6 YCTSLRA LAPEAC

Here are the away shirts of twelve Premier League and Championship clubs, but their team names have been jumbled up!

Can you figure out who's who?

7 OONEUMTBRUH

8 NQESEU RKAP GRARNES

9 KOETS TCIY

10 WESATNELC TUNEDI

11 ROTPENS HRTNO NDE

12 NATOS LAVIL

Magic MOMENT

Magic 45+4'

PLAY-OFF *Drama*

FIXTURE:	Sky Bet Championship Play-Off semi-final first leg
DATE:	Saturday, 9 May 2015
SCORE:	Ipswich Town 1 Norwich City 1
VENUE:	Portman Road
ATTENDANCE:	29,166

Town sealed a sixth place Championship finish in 2014/15. And that in turn, set up an East Anglian derby meeting with Norwich City in the play-offs.

Although Town had suffered defeat in their previous four derby matches, Mick McCarthy's men stopped the rot following a keenly-contested Portman Road clash.

The visitors took a 41st minute lead but Town were not to be defeated on this occasion, and deep into first-half injury-time the home fans among a crowd of almost 30,000 went wild as Paul Anderson fired home a memorable equaliser in front of the Sir Alf Ramsey Stand. The goal left the tie perfectly balanced for the second leg.

25

TAYO
EDUN

59

How's your knowledge of the laws of the game?

You think you can do better than the man in the middle?
here's your chance to prove it...

HEY REF!

1. Kayden Jackson shoots for goal from 25 yards. His fierce drive deflects off your head, wrong-footing the keeper, on its way into the back of the net. What's your call?

A: You award an indirect free-kick to the opposition.
B: It's a goal!
C: You give a drop-ball from where you were hit with ball.

2. Ellis Harrison strikes for goal from six yards, but as he shoots, the ball bursts and stops just before the goal line. Alert, he follows up and taps the ball home. What's your call?

A: It's a goal!
B: You award a penalty kick to the Blues.
C: No goal and you restart with a drop ball where the ball burst.

3. Kayden Jackson sends the keeper the wrong way from the penalty spot, but his effort hits the post and rebounds straight to Ellis Harrison who rifles the ball into the net to score. What is your decision?

A: It's a goal!
B: The spot kick has to be retaken.
C: You award an indirect free-kick to the opposition.

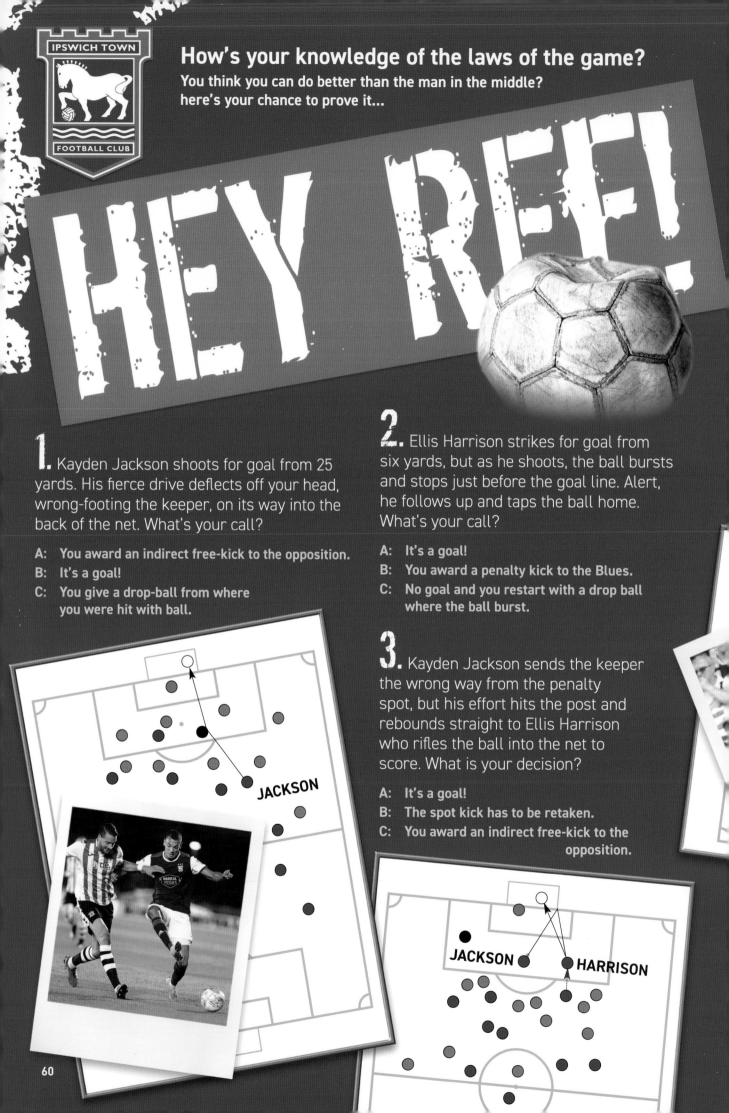

JACKSON

JACKSON   HARRISON

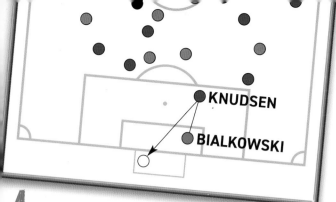

4. Bartosz Bialkowski attempts to take a quick goal kick, but to his horror, it hits Jonas Knudsen who is still in the penalty area and the ball deflects into his own net. What's your call, ref?

A: It's a goal!

B: A corner kick to the opposing team

C: The goal kick has to be retaken.

5. Standing in his own penalty area, Bartosz Bialkowski catches the ball directly from teammate Jonas Knudsen's throw-in. What is your decision?

A: Everything's fine. Play on.

B: You award the opposing team an indirect free-kick.

C: A yellow card for Bialkowski and a penalty for the opposing team.

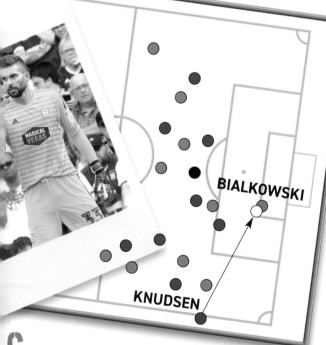

6. You have decided Kayden Jackson's spot kick must be re-taken after an infringement by the keeper. This time Ellis Harrison steps forward to take the kick. Is that allowed?

A: No, I award an indirect free kick to the opposition.

B: Yes, any Town player can re-take the penalty.

C: No, the player who took the initial spot kick, Kayden Jackson, must retake the kick.

7. You have awarded a drop ball. As you drop the ball, Jonas Knudsen and the opposing player both kick the ball at exactly the same time before it hits the turf. What's your ruling?

A: You show a yellow card to both players for ungentlemanly conduct.

B: You drop the ball again.

C: Play on.

8. Ellis Harrison is on the scoresheet again, tapping in from only three yards out. When he scores, he is slightly ahead of the last defender, but in line with the goalkeeper. What is your decision?

A: Goal. In line with the keeper is not offside.

B: Goal disallowed. Harrison is offside. To be onside, he must be in line with the second last opponent or the ball.

C: Goal. A player can't be offside inside the six-yard box.

9. Ellis Harrison takes a long throw in aiming for the head of Luke Chambers. No-one makes contact with the ball and it bounces into the net direct from Harrison's throw. What's your call, ref?

A: Goal. Providing there was an attempt to play the ball.

B: Goal. As long as the throw-in was taken correctly.

C: No Goal. A goal can never be scored direct from a throw in.

ANSWERS

PAGE 26 · FANTASTIC

Harry Kane, Jordan Pickford, Raheem Sterling, Jordan Henderson and Harry Maguire.

PAGE 34 · GUESS THE CLUB

1. Ajax. 2. Paris Saint-Germain. 3. Bayern Munich.
4. Sporting Lisbon. 5. Real Madrid. 6. Arsenal. 7. Celtic.
8. Juventus. 9. Barcelona. 10. Club Brugge

PAGE 40 · WHO ARE YER?

1. Dean Gerken. 2. Ellis Harrison. 3. Bartosz Bialkowski.
4. Cole Skuse. 5. Andre Dozzell. 6. Luke Chambers.
7. Freddie Sears. 8. Flynn Downes. 9. Gwion Edwards.
10. Jordan Roberts.

PAGE 45
2017/18 END OF TERM EXAM

1. Joe Garner. 2. Mustapha Carayol. 3. Bartosz Bialkowski,
45 appearances. 4. Ipswich Town 5 Sunderland 2. 5. 60.
6. Luton Town 0 Ipswich Town 2. 7. Birmingham City.
8. Martyn Waghorn, 11 yellow cards. 9. Martyn Waghorn.
10. 14.

PAGE 53 · SPOT THE BALL

PAGE 53 · WHAT BALL?

Ball H

PAGE 56 · HERO HUNT

Russell Osman

PAGE 57 · SHIRT SHUFFLE

1. Liverpool. 2. Fulham. 3. Sheffield United.
4. Birmingham City. 5. West Ham United. 6. Crystal Palace.
7. Bournemouth. 8. Queens Park Rangers. 9. Stoke City.
10. Newcastle United. 11. Preston North End. 12. Aston Villa.

PAGE 60 · HEY REF!

1. B. 2. C. 3. A. 4. C. 5. B. 6. B. 7. B. 8. B. 9. C.